Physical Education for CCEA GCSE

SECOND EDITION

Workbook ②

Derek Prentice

PE for CCEA GCSE

Contents

Introduction **p3**

Section 7: Effects **p4**

Section 8: Health & safety issues **p13**

Section 9: Exercise and training sessions **p16**

Section 10: Exercise and training programmes...................**p30**

Section 11: Individual performance in physical activities **p46**

PE for CCEA GCSE
Introduction

Purpose of this workbook

This workbook complements the textbook *Physical Education For CCEA GCSE Second Edition* by Derek Prentice (Colourpoint, 2009).

It will help you prepare for the terminal exam by:
- checking your knowledge and understanding of the facts, terminology, concepts, principles and methods included in the subject content and by getting you to make decisions in applying them;
- asking you to analyse, interpret, and evaluate information and material relating to the subject content;
- challenging you to write answers that are clear, concise and legible.

The knowledge and skills that you develop in completing this workbook will be relevant and contribute to your success in the other two components of the course.

How to use the workbook

1. Read over the questions and tasks set in this workbook for a Section in the textbook. This will give you an idea of what you will have to know, understand and be able to do.

2. Read the Section in the textbook. This will give you an overall view of the Section and let you discover where you will find the information for answering the questions and tasks in the workbook.

3. Answer the questions and tasks in the workbook for the Section.
   Note: Read each question and instruction carefully and make sure that the answers you write in the workbook are correct. Make a big effort to be clear and concise in your answers and ensure that your writing is legible. Do not copy the answers from other students as this will not help you learn.

4. The workbook provides opportunities for you to discuss your answers formally in class with the teacher and other students or informally outside class with other students and adults. This experience will provide you with feedback on your understanding of the questions and feedback on your ability to write your answers clearly and concisely.

Section 7 | PE for CCEA GCSE p76-92

Effects

The effects of exercise and training and physical activity on the body (p76–)

In this section be prepared to go back and forth between the body systems to find your answers.

7.1 The body systems work together to allow you to perform physical tasks, events or sports. The body systems that are most involved in this are given below. Draw simple diagrams to represent these systems.

The respiratory system	The circulatory system	The musculatory system

7.2 Muscles do the work. They produce the movement. They are the engine of the body. (p82)

Cardiac muscle moves _____

_____

Smooth muscle moves _____

_____

Skeletal muscle moves _____

Muscles need oxygen and nutrients to be able to work. How do they get their supply of oxygen? How do they produce the energy and what happens to the waste products?

7.3 Consider the process and write in the correct words below. (p76, 79)

The respiratory system transfers _____ from the outside air into the blood.

The circulatory system transports oxygen and _____ to the working muscles.

The musculatory system uses the _____ and _____ to produce energy.

The circulatory system transports the waste product _____ _____ to the lungs.

The respiratory system transfers the carbon dioxide from the _____ into the outside air.

4

7.4 Annotate (add notes to) the **diagrams** to explain **how** the **respiratory system gets oxygen** into the blood. (p77)

Inspiration	Diffusion
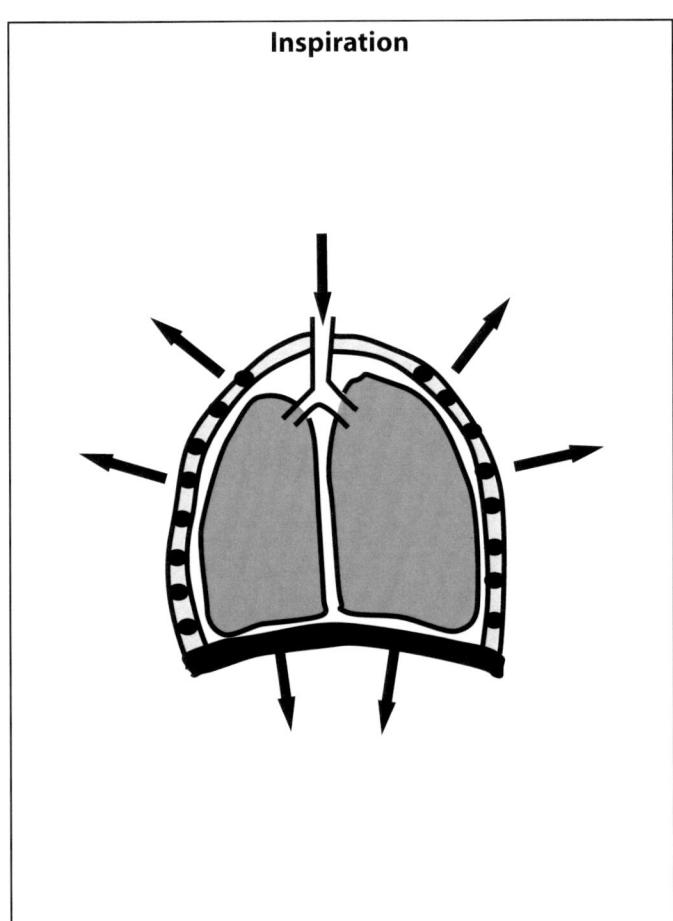	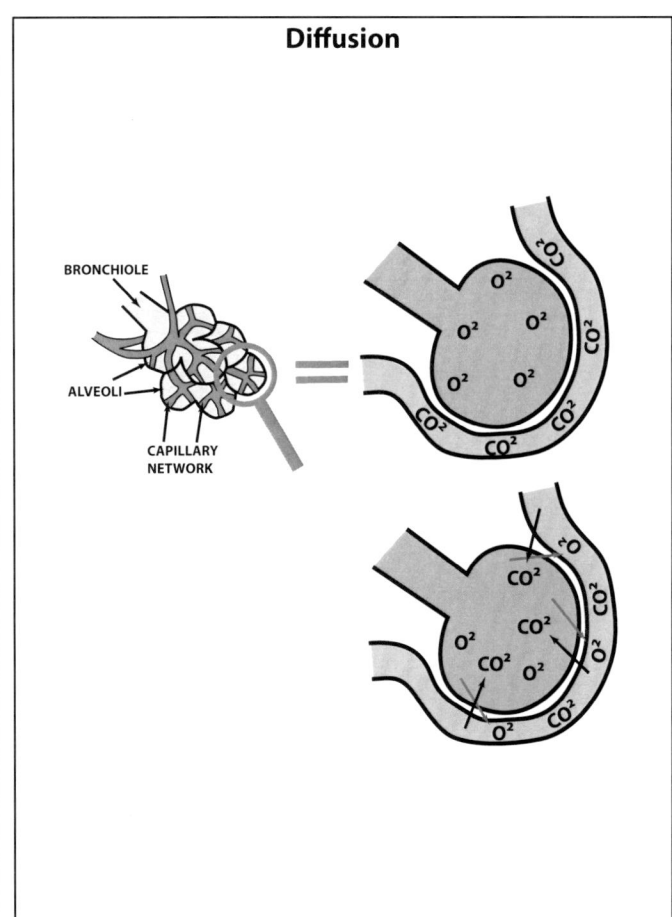

7.5 Annotate the **diagram** to explain **how** the **circulatory system delivers** the **oxygen** and **fuel** to the muscles and takes away the waste products. (p80)

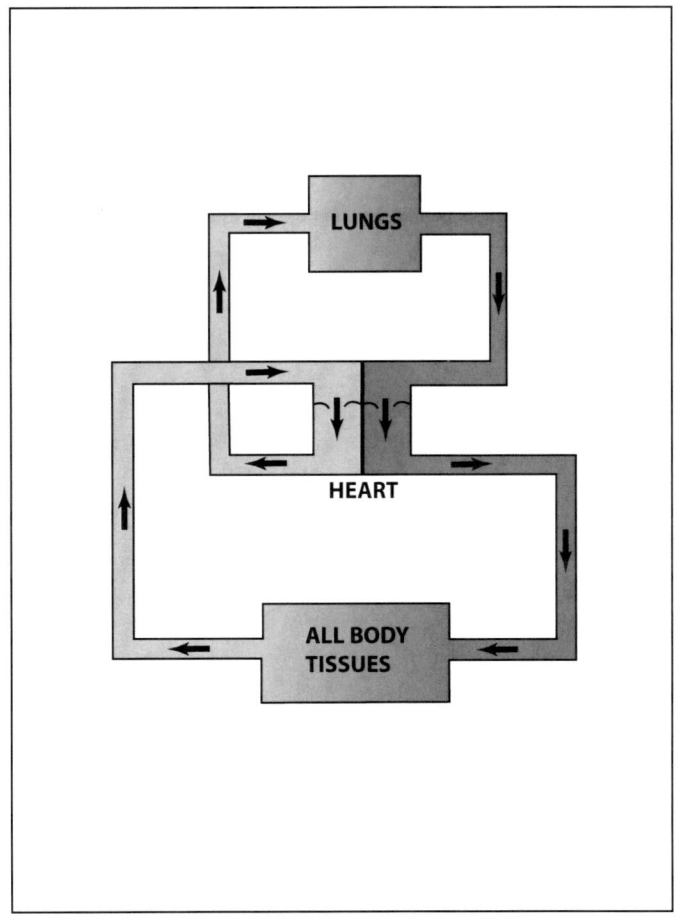

7.6 How does the muscle produce aerobic energy? Complete the paragraph below. (p85)

_____ and _____ are broken down to provide _____.

The waste products _____ from producing the energy are broken down by using

_____ and can be breathed out as _____ _____.

You can keep going using the _____ energy system until you run out of glycogen.

7.7 Factors influencing performance
Vital capacity and ventilation influence the performance of the respiratory system. (p78)

Vital capacity is _____

_____

_____

Ventilation is _____

_____

_____

7.8 Stroke volume and cardiac output influence the performance of the circulatory system. (Page 80)

Stroke volume is _____

_____

Cardiac output is _____

_____

Short-term or immediate effects of training on the body systems

When you start to exercise your muscles need more oxygen and more fuel.

7.9 Annotate the **diagrams** opposite to explain **how** the **respiratory system responds** to meet this extra demand.

At rest	During exercise
	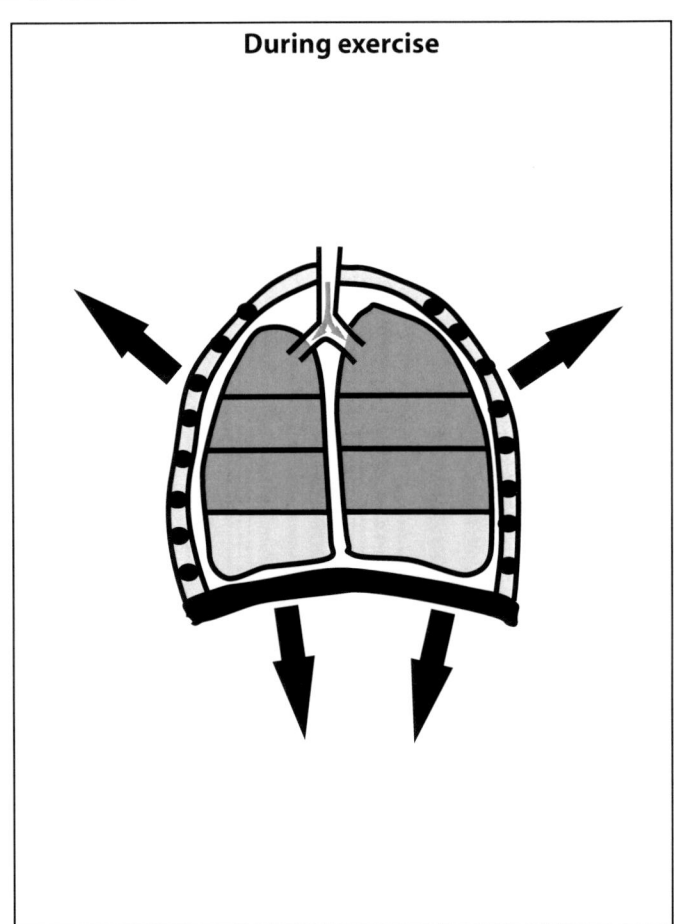

When you start to exercise your muscles need more oxygen and more fuel. (p81)

7.10 **Annotate** the **diagrams** below to explain **how** the **circulatory system responds** to meet this demand.

At rest	During exercise
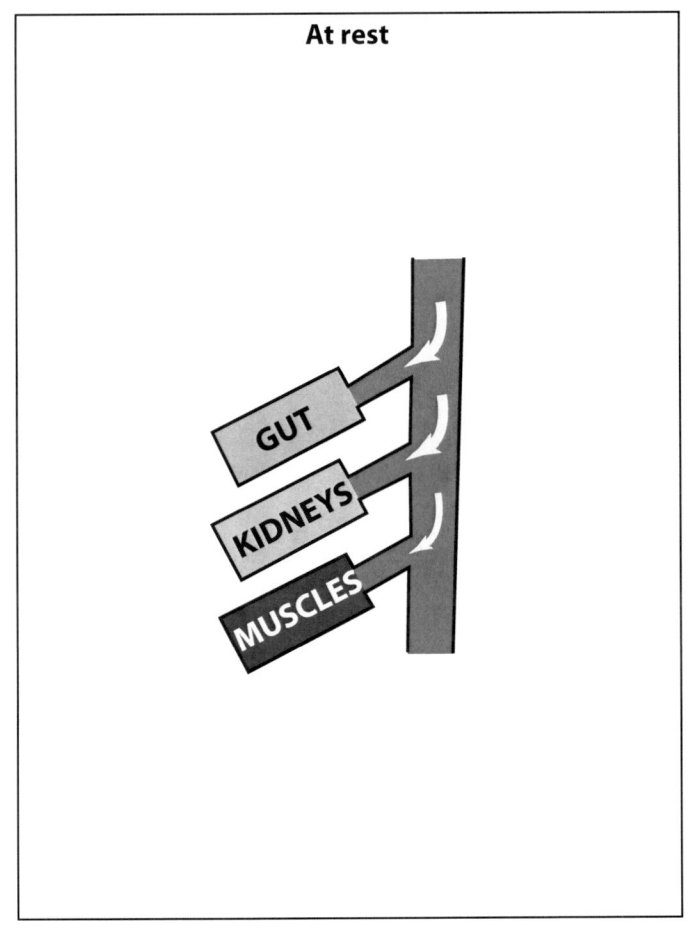	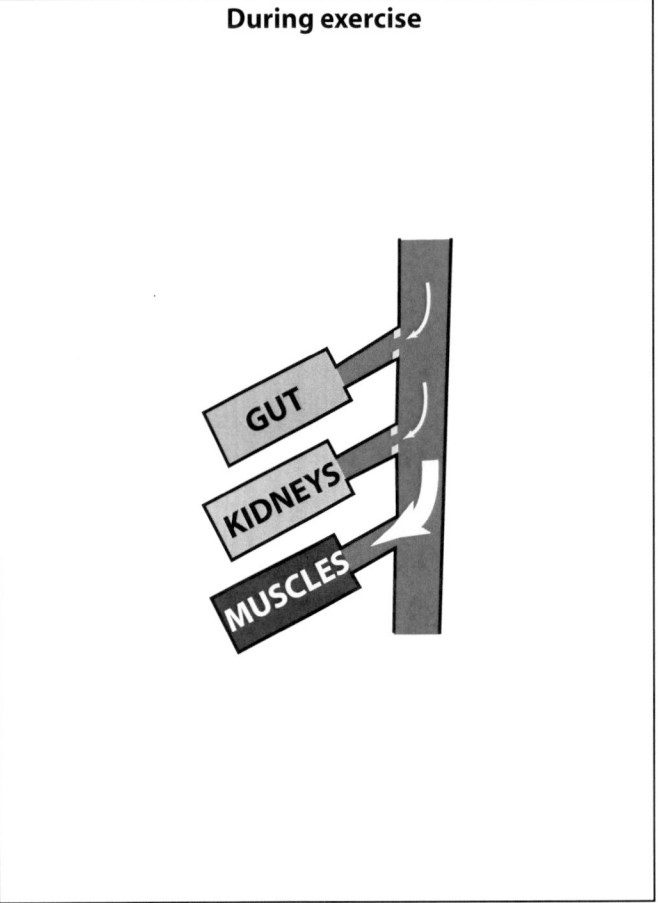

When you start to exercise your muscles need more oxygen and more fuel.

7.11 Annotate the diagrams below to explain how the musculatory system responds to meet this demand. (p81)

At rest	During exercise

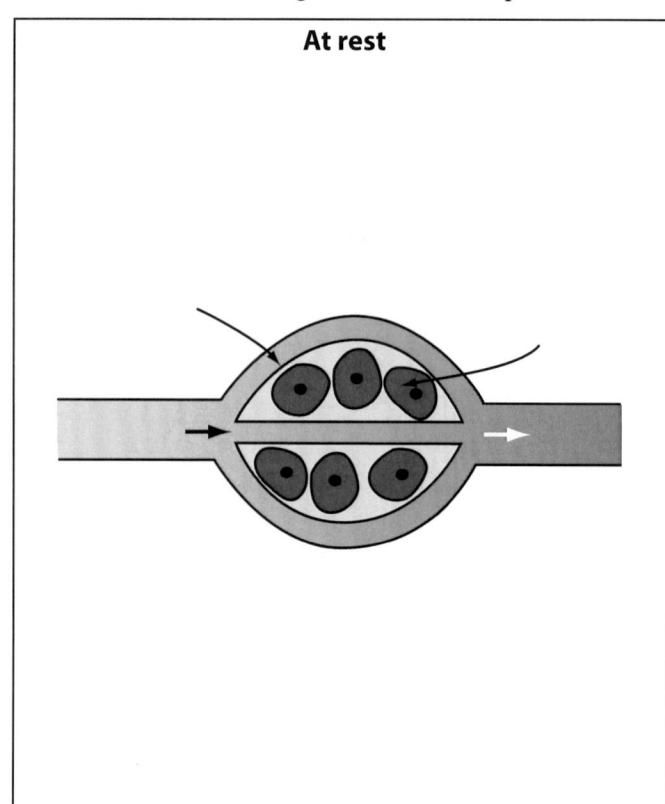
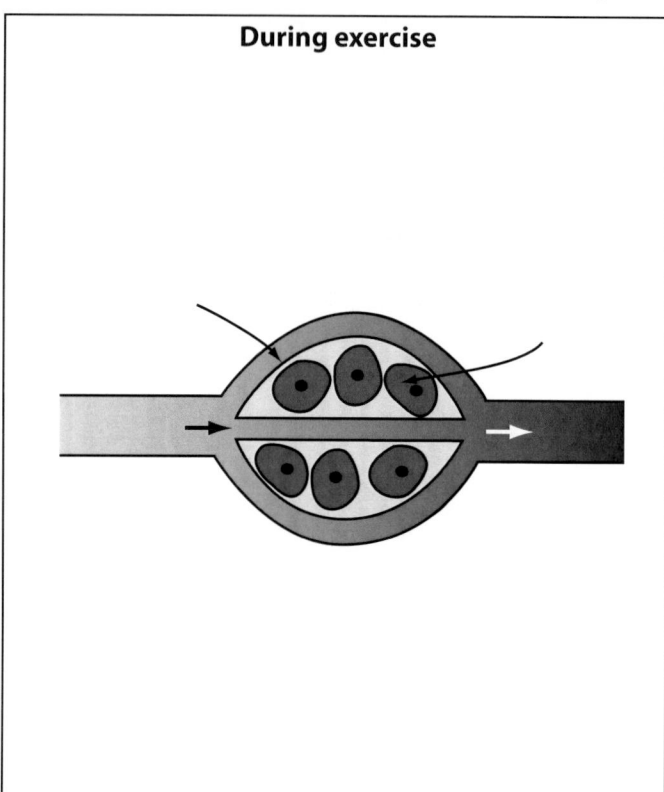

Long-term effects of training on the body systems

If you do appropriate and regular exercise/training your body systems such as the respiratory, circulatory and musculatory become more efficient. In other words you become fitter.

7.12 What physical changes take place in the respiratory system to make it more efficient? (p79)
Annotate the diagrams to explain the physical changes.

Unfit	Fit

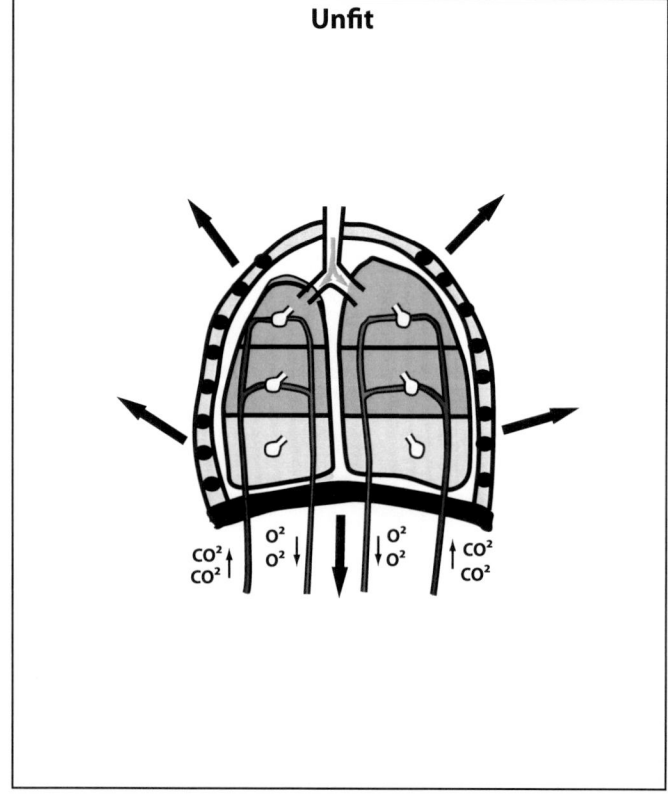
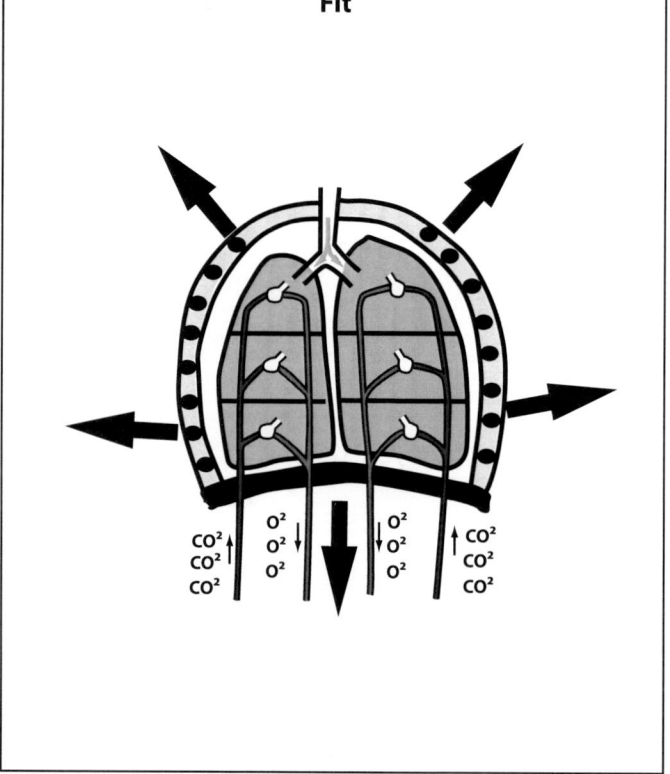

7.13 What **physical changes** take place in the **circulatory system** to make it **more efficient**? (p82)
Annotate the **diagrams** to explain the physical changes.

Unfit	Fit
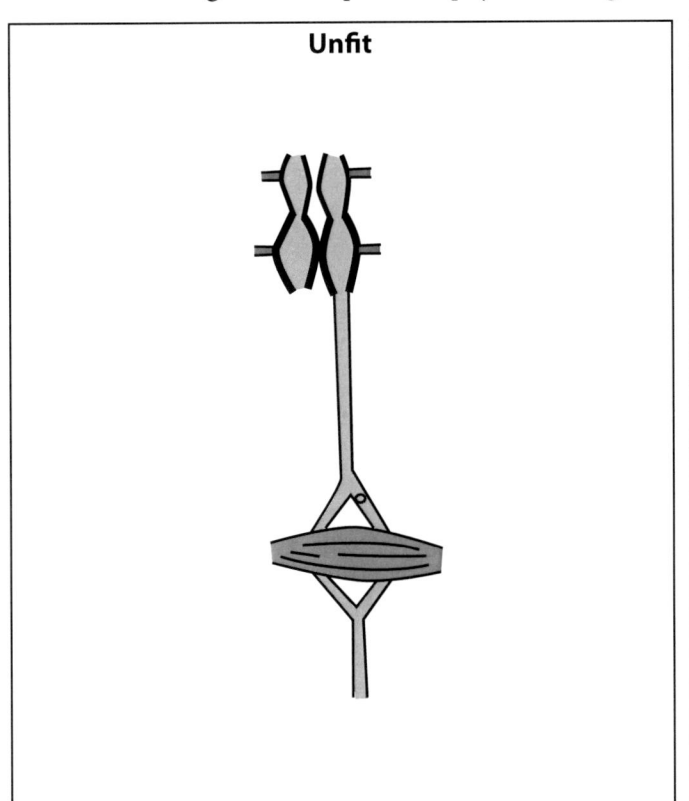	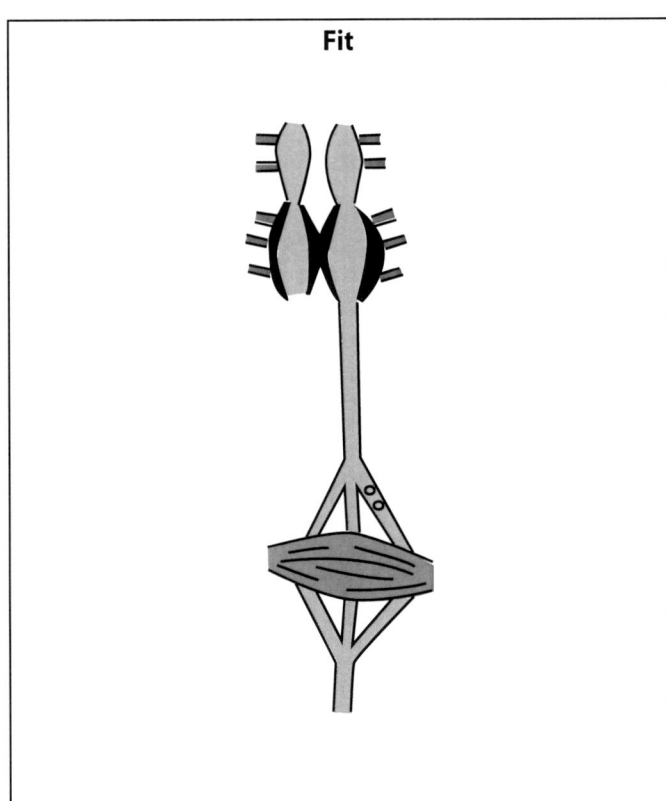

7.14 What **physical changes** take place in the **musculatory system** to make it **more efficient**? (p86)
Annotate the **diagrams** to explain the physical changes.

Aerobic fitness

Unfit	Fit
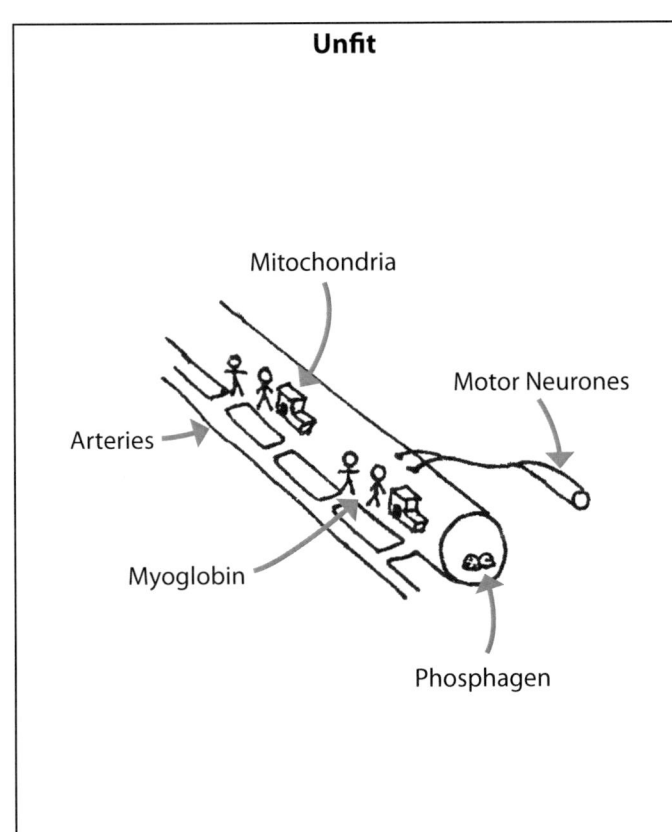	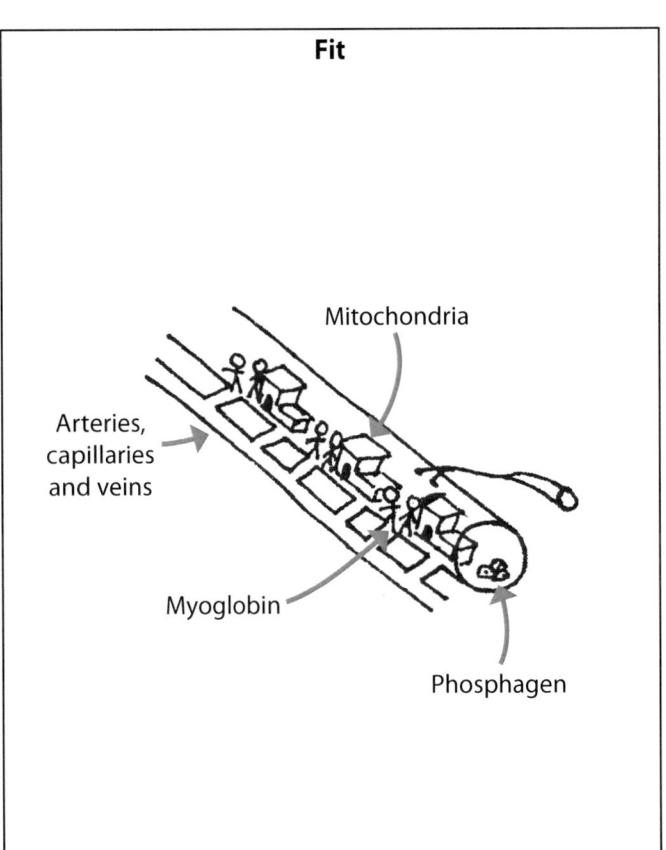

Muscular strength

Unfit

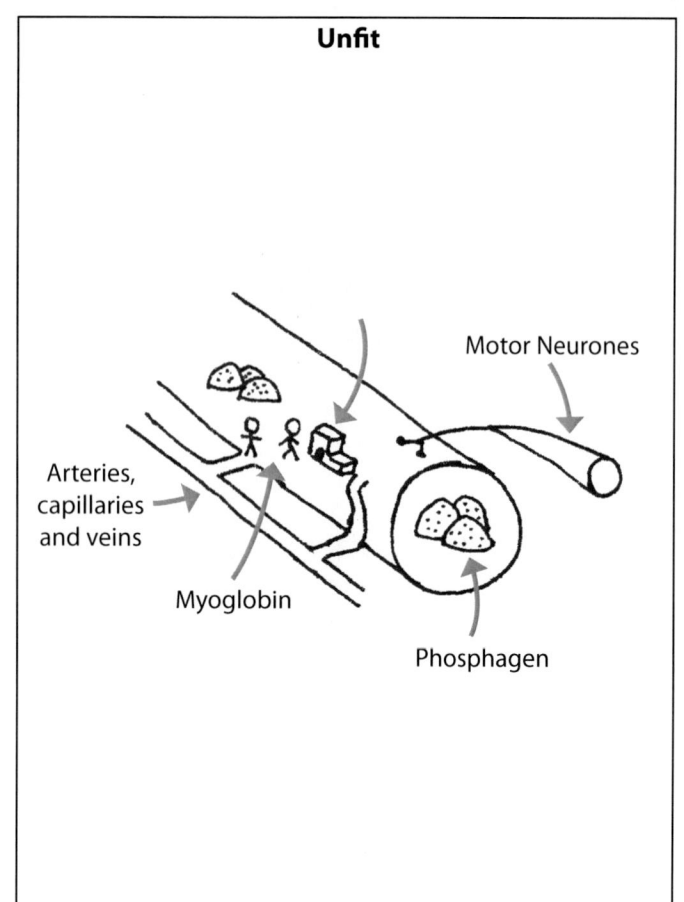

Fit

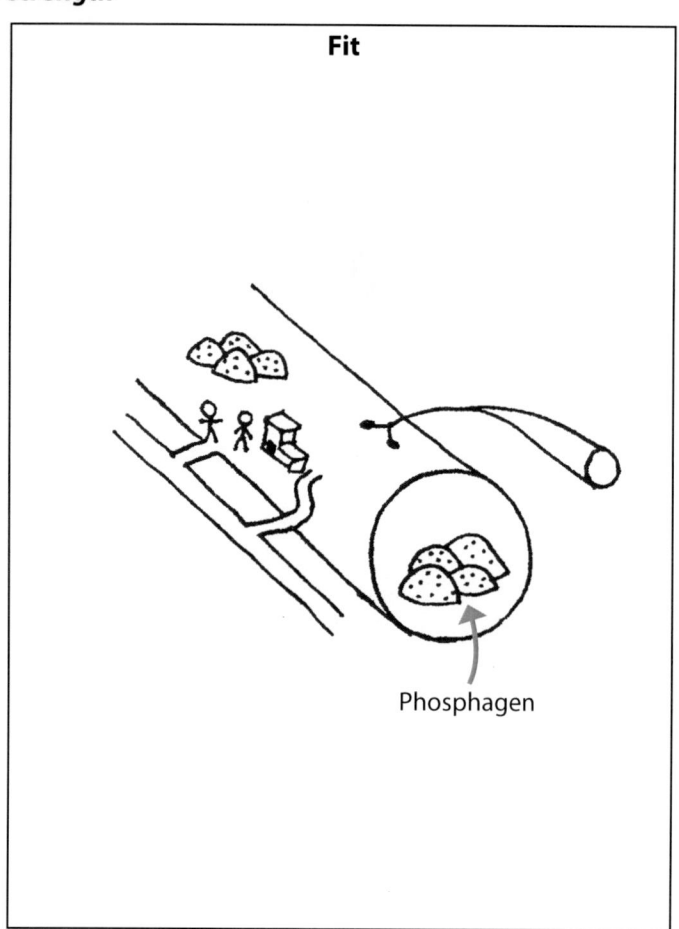

The physical changes in the body systems make them work more efficiently. Explain what this means practically for the following physical changes.

The intercostal muscles and diaphragm become stronger. (p79)

_____

_____

_____

More blood capillaries develop in the muscles. (p86)

_____

_____

_____

Increased stores of myoglobin. (p86)

_____

_____

_____

The muscles cannot work without the skeleton and digestive system.

The skeleton

It is the muscles pulling on the jointed skeleton that allows movement to take place.

7.15 **Name** one other **function** of the **skeleton** that is important **for aerobic fitness**. (p87)

___

7.16 **Explain** the short-term and long-term effects of exercise on the skeleton. (p89)

___

The digestive system

7.17 What is the role of the digestive system? (p90)

___

7.18 Complete the following: (p91)

Carbohydrates are broken down into _____

Proteins are broken down into _____

Fats are broken down into _____

7.19 Explain why it is wise not to eat before you exercise. (p91)

_____

_____

_____

_____

_____

_____

_____

_____

_____

_____

_____

Time To Spare?

If you have finished this section and are waiting for others to finish, try the wordsearch.

c	a	p	i	l	l	a	r	i	e	s	o	a
d	n	r	l	y	a	c	t	l	u	n	r	i
d	i	f	f	u	s	i	o	n	a	y	n	i
n	b	a	h	r	o	r	a	n	n	s	t	s
o	o	i	p	d	u	c	r	u	p	e	b	r
t	l	d	r	h	a	u	e	i	c	l	u	y
e	g	i	o	d	r	l	r	t	l	c	l	s
l	o	y	r	o	t	a	l	u	c	s	u	m
e	y	r	e	y	t	t	g	y	i	u	r	s
k	m	i	k	i	a	o	i	m	i	m	f	t
s	y	r	o	t	a	r	i	p	s	e	r	p
s	g	n	u	l	d	y	a	e	o	p	u	l
c	a	r	d	i	a	c	s	a	f	a	l	i

cardiac
circulatory
diaphragm
diffusion
inspiration
lungs
muscles
musculatory
respiratory
skeleton
capillaries
myoglobin

Section 8 | PE for CCEA GCSE p93–96
Health & safety issues

8.1 Complete the following paragraph from page 93.

_____ exercise is good for your _____. However, if it is done thoughtlessly it can become a _____ and cause _____ _____.

Safety must be a _____ when you exercise. By identifying _____ hazards you can take _____ to _____ the _____ of illness or injury occurring. Remember, _____ should always be your priority.

8.2 Extended writing

Explain what steps people should take to minimise the risks of illness, injury or possible death when they want to train really hard or compete at their potential.

In your answer cover at least six of the headings from Section 8.

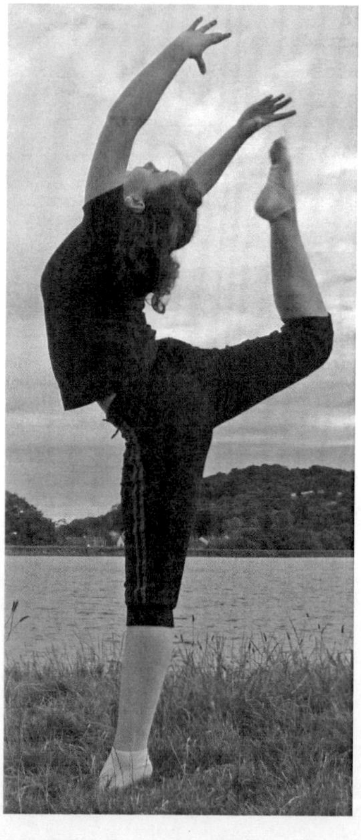

Time To Spare?

In our everyday lives we are surrounded by warning and information signs. For example, you have signs telling people to refrain from smoking or signs telling people not to dive into the swimming pool. Design signs of your own that warn or give information to people.

Section 9 | PE for CCEA GCSE p97–111

Exercise and training sessions

Planning a training session brings together much of what you have learnt in previous sections. It may be worth revisiting these sections when you are unsure of what choices to make. You will also be expected to look within this section for information and guidance. It will be like doing a jigsaw. You have to look for key pieces and place them correctly.

Exercise/training sessions are the building blocks for exercise/training programmes.

An exercise/training session normally has a warm-up, a workout and a cool-down. What is the **purpose** of each of these phases?

Warm-up (p98)	Workout (p102)	Cool-down (p108)
The purpose of the warm-up is to:	The purpose of the workout is to:	The purpose of the cool-down is to:

9.1 Planning a safe, appropriate and effective warm-up (p98–101)

9.1.1 A safe, appropriate and effective warm-up should include pulse-raising activity, mobility exercises and flexibility exercises. You have three decisions to make for each area in order for them to be safe and appropriate. What are the decisions?

Decisions to be made:

1 _____

2 _____

3 _____

16

9.1.2 Read 'Planning the pulse-raising activities', 'Planning the mobility exercises' and 'Planning the flexibility exercises' on pages 98–101. Then complete the following passage which outlines the warm-up for a reasonably fit group who want to play a competitive game of badminton. Use the words below to fill in the blanks so that the passage makes sense.

backwards	freely	short	rhythmically	hips
lifts	pulse-raising	skipping	kicking	dynamic
range	limbs	tension	arms	ankle
knee	practise	shoulders	shots	static
limit	mobility	wearing	sweat	temperature
gently	jogging	warm-up	warm	fits

The _____

I would choose _____ as the first pulse-raising activity as it _____ in with the game of badminton. I would have the group jog until they felt _____ and were starting to _____ slightly. This could be for 7–10 minutes depending on what they were _____ and on the outside _____. I would then introduce other exercises on the feet that were both _____ and _____. For example, _____ along to loosen-up the _____ joints, _____ the heels off the bottom to loosen-up the _____ joints, controlled high knee _____ to loosen-up the _____ and side skipping bringing both _____ up above the head to loosen-up the _____ and hips. These exercises, along with others, will keep the pulse up and the body temperature high. Other mobility exercises may be done while standing, for example, 'rolling' the shoulders or circling the hips. In all the mobility exercises the _____ are moved gently and _____ within their normal _____ of movement. The mobility exercises will be performed for _____ periods of time until the joints are moving _____. After the pulse-raising and mobility exercises I would use a range of _____ flexibility exercises to _____ stretch the major muscles. The muscles should be slowly stretched to their _____ and held under mild _____ for 5–15 seconds.

I would then get the people to jog and then to gradually perform more _____ movements on court, for example, moving forwards, _____, sideways and jumping. These movements would be similar to what they would have to perform in the badminton game.

Finally, I would get them to _____ their range of badminton _____.

9.1.3 Read 'Evaluating the safety, appropriateness and effectiveness of a warm-up' on page 101, then apply the four steps to **evaluate** the **warm-up** that is described in the previous task.

_____

_____

_____

_____

_____

_____

_____

_____

_____

_____

_____

_____

_____

_____

_____

_____

_____

9.1.4 Use **stick diagrams** and the minimum of **annotation** to **explain** how you should perform two different **mobility exercises**.

9.2 Planning a safe, appropriate and effective workout (p102–107)

Planning to develop the aerobic or anaerobic energy systems (p102–104)

9.2.1 There are three major decisions that you have to get right to plan a safe, appropriate and effective workout to develop aerobic or anaerobic energy production. What are these three decisions?

1 _____

2 _____

3 _____

9.2.2 Consider the following individuals and their circumstances. **Match** the **options** given for physical activities, training methods, intensities and times **to** the appropriate **individuals** and their circumstances.

Be prepared to explain your decisions.

Running; Swimming; Cycling; Somewhat hard; Hard; Fairly hard;

Continuous steady pace; Fartlek; 60 minutes; 20 minutes; 40 minutes

Aerobic fitness	A teenager who is grossly overweight, but is not embarrassed about it	A reasonably fit 20 year-old who wants better aerobic fitness	An active senior citizen who lives 6 miles from the nearest village
Physical activity			
Training method			
Intensity			
Time			

9.2.3 Using the options above, **decide** what would be **most suitable** for the following individuals and their circumstances.

Be prepared to explain your decisions.

Aerobic fitness	A physically fit teenager who plays team sports	An active middle-aged lady who loves water	A person who owns a dog
Physical activity			
Training method			
Intensity			
Time			

Interval training can be used to develop aerobic or anaerobic fitness. It depends on how it is used.
In both aerobic and anaerobic workouts the intensity is mostly given as a percentage of maximum heart rate.

How to calculate a percentage of maximum heart rate

1. The maximum heart rate can be obtained by subtracting the person's age from 220 (for men) and 226 (for women).
2. Multiply the maximum heart rate by whatever percentage would be appropriate for the person.

For a 20 year old man to exercise at 70% of his maximum heart rate (MHR):
1. Subtract 20 from 220. 220 − 20 = 200. This is his maximum heart rate (MHR).
2. Multiply 200 × 70%. This is 200 × 0.70. 200 × 0.7 = 140. 70% of a 20 year old man's maximum heart rate (MHR) is 140 beats per minute.

9.2.4 Calculate your own target heart rate zone to develop aerobic fitness (70 – 90%MHR).

To calculate my maximum heart rate (MHR) I subtract my age from 220 (for boys) or 226 (for girls).

226 or 220 − ☐ = ☐   My maximum heart rate is ☐ beats per minute.

The minimum intensity for me would be 70% of my MHR.

To calculate this I multiply my MHR by 0.70.   ☐ MHR × 0.7 = ☐

The lower end of my target heart rate zone is ☐ beats per minute.

The maximum intensity for me would be 90% of my MHR.

To calculate this I multiply my MHR by 0.90.   ☐ MHR × 0.9 = ☐

The upper end of my target heart rate zone is ☐ beats per minute.

Anaerobic fitness
For me to work above the anaerobic threshold my heart rate must be above ☐ beats per minute.

9.2.5 Calculate the target heart rate zones for aerobic exercise for the following individuals. Take 70% of maximum heart rate (MHR) as the aerobic threshold and 90%MHR as the anaerobic threshold.

A 30 year old female	A 60 year old male
Target heart rate zone:	Target heart rate zone:

9.2.6 Read pages 52–53 again. Use this information and your ability to calculate percentages of maximum heart rates to show the differences between using **interval training** (on a 400m running track) to **develop aerobic** fitness and **interval training** to **develop anaerobic** fitness. The athlete is female and 26 years old.

Decisions to be made for interval training	Interval training to develop aerobic fitness (female athlete 26 years old)	Interval training to develop anaerobic fitness (female athlete 26 years old)
Decision on intensity (%MHR and heart rates)		
Decision on work time		
Decision on number of repetitions		
Decision on recovery time between repetitions		
Decision on number of sets		
Decision on recovery time between sets		

Explanation of my decisions:

_____
_____
_____
_____
_____
_____
_____
_____
_____
_____

Planning to develop muscular fitness – power, strength, speed and endurance (p105 –107)

9.2.7 What are the **five** decisions that you have to make to plan a safe, appropriate and effective workout to develop muscular fitness – power, strength, speed and endurance? (p105)

1 _____

2 _____

3 _____

4 _____

5 _____

9.2.8 What are the **advantages** of using **weight training** to improve muscular fitness compared to using circuit training or assault-course-type training? (p105)

_____

_____

_____

_____

_____

_____

_____

_____

9.2.9 Why are the **exercises** for the different parts of the body done **in rotation**? (p105)

_____

_____

_____

_____

_____

It is important that you have a bank of safe and appropriate weight training and circuit training exercises to develop muscular fitness in the upper body (arms and chest), trunk (stomach and back) and lower body (hips and legs).

9.2.10 Choose one **safe**, **appropriate** and **effective weight training exercise** and one **safe**, **appropriate** and **effective circuit training exercise** for each of the **upper body, trunk** and **lower body**. Use **stick diagrams** and **words** to show **how** each should be **performed**.

Choose different exercises from the ones you chose in Workbook 1 Section 4.

Weight training exercise for the **upper body**	**Circuit training exercise** for the **upper body**

Weight training exercise for the **trunk**	**Circuit training exercise** for the **trunk**

Weight training exercise for the **lower body**	**Circuit training exercise** for the **lower body**

Study the tables again on page 58 of the textbook to help you understand the intensities to be used for the range of muscular fitness components, the number of repetitions, the number of sets and the recovery times between sets.

9.2.11 Evaluate the following options.

Which **option** is most **appropriate** for developing **muscular strength**? **Explain** your choice.

Weight training	Option 1	Option 2	Option 3
Weight	8RM	10RM	15RM
Number of repetitions	6 repetitions	12 repetitions	12 repetitions
Number of sets	4 sets	3 sets	4 sets
Rest between sets	3 minutes	2 minutes	3 minutes

I believe that **Option** _____ is **most appropriate** for developing **muscular strength**.

Explanation: _____

_____

_____

_____

9.2.12 Evaluate the following options.

Which **option** is most **appropriate** for developing **muscular power**? **Explain** your choice.

Weight training	Option 1	Option 2	Option 3
Weight	80% of 1RM	3RM	90% of 1RM
Number of repetitions	5 repetitions	3 repetitions	3 repetitions
Number of sets	4 sets	3 sets	4 sets
Rest between sets	4 minutes	1 minute	3 minutes

I believe that **Option** _____ is **most appropriate** for developing **muscular power**.

Explanation: _____

_____

_____

_____

9.2.13 Evaluate the following options.

Which **option** is most **appropriate** for developing **muscular endurance**? **Explain** your choice.

Circuit training	Option 1	Option 2	Option 3
Intensity	Somewhat hard	Somewhat hard	Hard
Number of repetitions	20 repetitions	25 repetitions	15 repetitions
Number of sets	2 sets	3 sets	4 sets
Rest between sets	30 seconds	3 minutes	1 minute

I believe that **Option** _____ is **most appropriate** for developing **muscular endurance**.

Explanation: _____

_____

_____

9.2.14 Evaluate the following options.

Which **option** is most **appropriate** for developing **muscular speed**? **Explain** your choice.

Training	Option 1	Option 2	Option 3
Intensity	Somewhat hard	Easy	Hard
Number of repetitions	20 repetitions	25 repetitions	15 repetitions
Number of sets	2 sets	1 set	1 set
Rest between sets	3 minutes	No rest	No rest

I believe that **Option** _____ is **most appropriate** for developing **muscular speed**.

Explanation: _____

_____

_____

9.2.15 Choose **six** safe and appropriate **circuit training exercises** (no weights) to cover the major areas of the body. The exercises should be suitable for **developing muscular endurance** and/or **aerobic fitness**. **Choose** the **order** in which the exercises should be done, the **work-time** for the exercises, the **recovery time** between each exercise and the rest time between each circuit.

Exercises	Worktime at each exercise	Recovery time between the exercises	Number of circuits	Rest time between each circuit
1				
2				
3				
4				
5				
6				

Planning to develop flexibility (p107)

9.2.16 If most people do not plan specific workouts for developing flexibility, when is flexibility developed?

_____

_____

9.3 Planning a safe, appropriate and effective cool-down (p108–111)

A cool-down normally includes pulse-lowering activities and flexibility exercises.

9.3.1 What happens to the body during the pulse-lowering activity in a cool-down? (p108)

_____

_____

_____

_____

_____

_____

_____

9.3.2 Why is it best to develop flexibility during the cool-down period? (p108)

_____

_____

_____

Planning to develop flexibility *(p109–110)*

Intensities and times for developing flexibility

With static flexibility exercises you slowly stretch the muscle to its normal limit and then stretch it a little further until it is under mild tension. You then hold the muscle in the stretched position for 30–60 seconds if your purpose is to develop flexibility.

9.3.3 Choose **safe** and **appropriate static flexibility** exercises for the upper body (neck, shoulders, chest and arms), the trunk (stomach, back and sides) and the lower body (hips and legs). **Describe** and use **stick diagrams** to show how the static flexibility exercises should be performed.

Static flexibility exercise for the **neck**	Static flexibility exercise for the **shoulders**

Static flexibility exercise for the **chest**	Static flexibility exercise for the **arms**

Static flexibility exercise for the **trunk**	Static flexibility exercise for the **trunk**
Static flexibility exercise for the **hips**	Static flexibility exercise for the **upper leg**
Static flexibility exercise for the **upper leg**	Static flexibility exercise for the **lower leg**

Time To Spare?

If you have finished this section and are waiting for others to finish, try the wordsearch.

p	l	a	n	n	i	n	g	c	u	r	t	o	r	r
n	w	t	t	s	n	t	s	l	s	m	i	s	m	a
e	f	f	e	c	t	i	v	e	i	p	i	a	o	u
i	s	t	i	m	e	p	a	i	n	i	n	f	b	a
v	t	a	p	p	r	o	p	r	i	a	t	e	i	v
n	e	e	p	e	v	a	l	u	a	t	e	t	l	n
p	l	t	t	r	a	i	n	i	n	g	n	y	i	s
u	i	c	o	o	l	d	o	w	n	t	s	e	t	s
r	r	a	e	o	t	s	o	f	i	l	i	t	y	w
p	n	e	x	e	r	c	i	s	e	s	t	t	k	o
o	l	i	p	w	a	r	m	u	p	m	y	a	i	r
s	f	l	e	x	i	b	i	l	i	t	y	a	a	k
e	i	o	y	a	n	f	e	a	m	p	s	x	b	o
r	e	p	e	t	i	t	i	o	n	s	a	f	e	u
e	i	r	r	f	n	e	e	p	p	v	t	m	d	t
n	e	p	a	t	g	o	a	l	s	n	t	p	t	o

cool down	sets	workout
evaluate	interval training	goals
warm up	exercises	training
flexibility	planning	repetitions
intensity	safety	purpose
mobility	time	effective
safe	appropriate	

Section 10 | PE for CCEA GCSE p112-139

Exercise and training programmes

What is an exercise or training programme? _____

_____

_____

_____

_____

_____

You are going to be asked to plan exercise/training programmes. To do this you should follow the guidance given in Section 8. You may also need to refer back to previous sections to help you.

10.1 Planning a weekly health-related exercise programme (p113–123)

10.1.1 Show that you can **follow the six steps** for planning a safe, appropriate and effective **weekly health-related exercise programme**.

Your challenge is to take someone from doing no exercise to doing the minimum amount of exercise to gain a health benefit in 4 weeks (see the FITT principle at the top of page 114).

Make the exercise programme as straightforward as you can.

Use the table on the next two pages.

Week	Monday	Tuesday	Wednesday	Thursday	Friday	Saturday	Sunday
1							
2							

Week	Monday	Tuesday	Wednesday	Thursday	Friday	Saturday	Sunday
3							
4							

10.1.2 Evaluating your present exercise/training programme.

First complete the table below to show what aerobic, muscular endurance and flexibility exercises you do on a regular basis. Make sure you provide the details necessary to allow you to complete a sound and accurate evaluation.

	Details of aerobic exercise	Details of muscular endurance exercise	Details of flexibility exercise
Sun			
Mon			
Tue			
Wed			
Thu			
Fri			
Sat			

Follow the steps on page 124 and 125 to evaluate your present exercise/training programme for maintaining good health.

_____
_____
_____
_____
_____
_____
_____
_____
_____
_____
_____

10.1.3 Evaluate the following as a safe, appropriate and effective **weekly health-related exercise programme**. Use the tables on page 114 to help you.

CSP = Continuous steady pace training

Mondays	Tuesdays	Wednesdays	Thursdays	Fridays	Saturdays	Sundays
	Swim CSP 75%MHR 30 minutes		Cycle CSP 70%MHR 30 minutes Weights 2 sets × 15 reps × 20RM		Run CSP 80%MHR 10 minutes Weights 2 sets × 15 reps × 20RM	Walk CSP 60%MHR 60 minutes

_____
_____
_____
_____
_____
_____

The **'full marks' health-related model** for GCSE PE is:

Aerobic – 6 workouts per week; moderate to hard intensity and an average of 30 minutes per workout.

Muscular endurance – 4 workouts per week; intensity moderate to hard; cover major muscle groups.

Flexibility – 6 'workouts' per week; intensity mild tension; stretches held for 30 seconds; cover major joints.

10.1.4 Plan a **health-related exercise programme** that takes the person from what is given as the overload for Week 1 up to the 'full marks' model by Week 8.

Tip: You have a goal for Week 8 (full marks model) so you could write in what you intend to be realistically doing in that week. This will help you to work out how to build up the training gradually over the weeks.

Use the table on the next four pages.

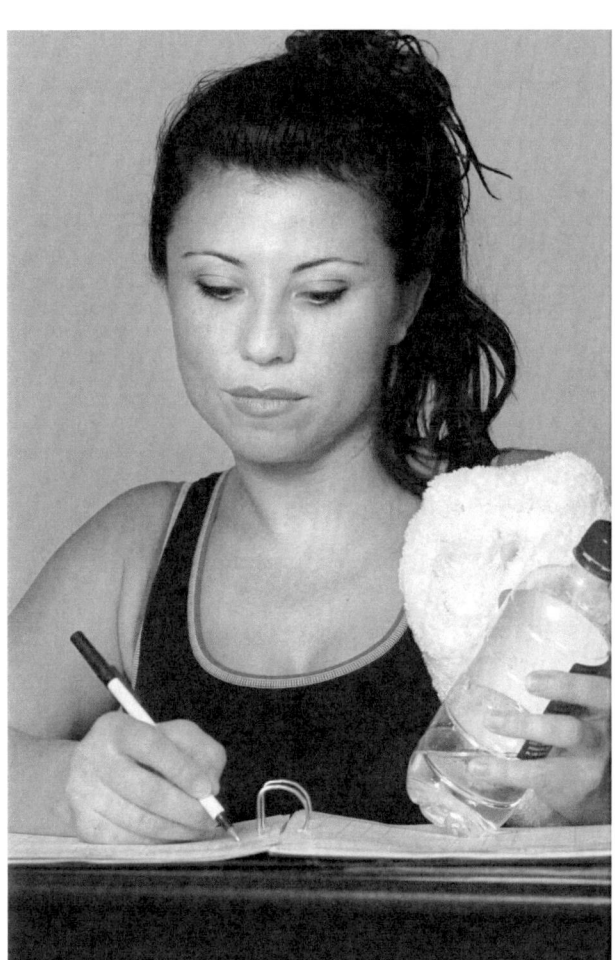

Week	Monday	Tuesday	Wednesday	Thursday	Friday	Saturday	Sunday
1		Run CSP 75%MHR 20 minutes. Static flexibility exercises - hold for 20 seconds.		Run CSP 70%MHR 30 minutes. Static flexibility exercises - hold for 20 seconds.		Cycle CSP 70%MHR 60 minutes. Static flexibility exercises - hold for 20 seconds.	
2							

Week	Monday	Tuesday	Wednesday	Thursday	Friday	Saturday	Sunday
3							
4							

Week	Monday	Tuesday	Wednesday	Thursday	Friday	Saturday	Sunday
5							
6							

Week	Monday	Tuesday	Wednesday	Thursday	Friday	Saturday	Sunday
7							
8							

10.2 Planning a training programme to develop peak physical fitness for events, sports or positions within sports

In planning a training programme for peak physical fitness you follow seven steps. These steps are similar to those for planning a health-related exercise programme. However, what you have to consider and the decisions you have to make are often more complex.

Read about how you apply the seven steps on pages 125–128. In addition to this, read how the SMARTER principle can help you check that your decisions are appropriate and effective (page 128). When you understand all of this, study the example of the training programme (Pages 128–129) and the explanations of the decisions made in planning it (p130–134). When you have done this, answer **10.2.1** below.

10.2.1 Take each of the seven steps in turn and **evaluate** how well each step has been applied to your training programmes/experiences for competitive events/sports. Provide evidence to support your evaluations.

Step 1: Applying the principle of specificity _____

_____

_____

Step 2: Applying the principle of variety _____

_____

_____

Step 3: Applying the principle of overload _____

_____

_____

Step 4: Applying the principle of progressive overload _____

_____

_____

Step 5: Applying the principle of rest/recovery _____

_____

_____

Step 6: Applying the principle of peaking _____

_____

_____

Step 7: Applying the principle of maintenance _____

_____

_____

10.2.2 Study the example of planning a training programme for a specific event. (pages 128–134 give the profile; the challenge; the training programme; the explanations for the decisions and the application of the SMARTER principle.)

Having successfully run the 10 km in 40 minutes, the person feels that they could do an even better time and agrees with you that a target of 38 minutes for the next 10 km race would be realistic. You have a further six weeks to prepare the person. Go through the process of planning the six weeks of training for the person. Explain your decisions.

Week	Sunday	Monday	Tuesday	Wednesday	Thursday	Friday	Saturday
1	Run 6 km 4:30 min/km 27 mins (Recovery)	Rest	Run 10 km 4:15 min/km 42 mins	Fartlek run 35 mins	Run 15 km 4:20min/km 65 mins	Run 7 km 4:00 min/km 28 mins	Run 15 km 4:20 min/km 65 mins
2							
3							
4							
5							
6							

10.3 Progressive overload

How to apply the principle of progressive overload to aerobic and anaerobic energy production workouts
(p134–136)

10.3.1 Show that you understand how to apply the principle of **progressive overload** to a training programme to improve **aerobic** or **anaerobic** fitness when using **interval training** as your training method.

The interval training workouts are in a swimming pool.

Interval training to improve aerobic fitness				Interval training to improve anaerobic fitness			
Repetitions	Distance	Work time	Recovery	Repetitions	Distance	Work time	Recovery
10 reps.	100m	72 sec.	1 min.	5 reps.	100m	64 sec.	5 min.

Explanation:	Explanation:

10.3.2 Study each of the following interval training workouts done on a 400m running track. State whether you believe the workouts are to develop aerobic fitness or anaerobic fitness. Explain your decisions.

Repetitions	Distance	Work time	Recovery	Repetitions	Distance	Work time	Recovery
20 reps.	100m	20 sec.	20 sec.	3 reps.	800m	3 min.	3 min.
This interval training workout is to improve _____ fitness. Explanation:				**This interval training workout is to improve _____ fitness.** Explanation:			

How to apply the principle of progressive overload to muscular fitness workouts (p136–138)

10.3.3 Show that you understand how to apply the principle of **progressive overload** to a training programme to improve **muscular strength** or **muscular endurance** when using **weight training** as your training method.

Weight training to improve muscular strength				Weight training to improve muscular endurance			
Sets	Repetitions	Weight	Recovery	Sets	Repetitions	Weight	Recovery
2 sets.	8 reps.	60kg	3 min.	2 sets.	15 reps.	30kg	60 sec.

10.3.4 Study the table below that shows how progressive overload can be applied to a training programme to develop muscular strength and to develop muscular endurance.

Weight training to improve muscular strength				Weight training to improve muscular endurance			
Sets	**Repetitions**	**Weight**	**Recovery**	**Sets**	**Repetitions**	**Weight**	**Recovery**
2 sets.	8 reps.	10RM	3 min.	2 sets.	20 reps.	20RM	60 sec.
2 sets.	8 reps.	10RM	3 min.	2 sets.	20 reps.	20RM	60 sec.
2 sets.	8 reps.	10RM	3 min.	2 sets.	20 reps.	20RM	60 sec.
2 sets.	8 reps.	10RM	3 min.	2 sets.	20 reps.	20RM	60 sec.
2 sets.	8 reps.	10RM	3 min.	2 sets.	20 reps.	20RM	60 sec.

Explain what must happen during these training programmes to make them effective.

_____

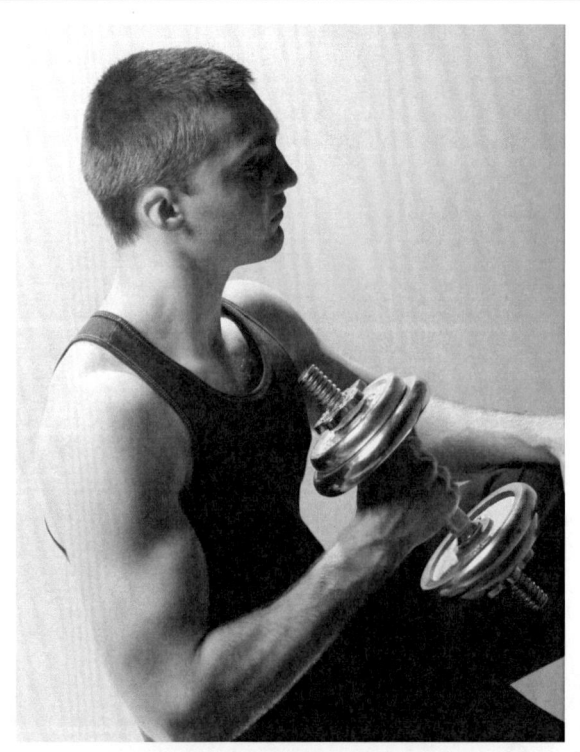

Time To Spare?

Use this page to design a poster for a specific event. The poster should attract people's attention; get them interested in going to, or entering the event, and finally give them the information they need (where the event is to take place; when it is to take place; what it will cost to go/enter and who to contact – giving web address, email address and telephone number).

Section 11 | PE for CCEA GCSE p140–157

Individual performance in physical activities

11.1 Skilled performance (p141)

11.1.1 **Underline** the **key words** in the following definitions.

Skilled performance or skill is the learnt ability to bring about a predetermined goal or result with maximum certainty and efficiency.

Skill is the ability to economically coordinate and control the movement to achieve the task goal.

11.1.2 Complete the sentences using one of the following terms.

coordinated and controlled   consistently   ability   goal/task/outcome   learned   economically/efficiently

Skill or skilled performance is _____ by the person.

Skill or skilled performance is an _____ to do something.

Skill or skilled performance has a predetermined _____.

The technique of the skill will be performed _____.

The sequence of movements of the skill will be _____.

The person will be _____ successful in performing the skill.

11.2 Cognitive, perceptual, motor, and perceptual motor skills (p141–142)

11.2.1 In many sports perceptual motor skills are important. **Describe** an **example** from a sport that **demonstrates** the use of **perceptual motor skills**.

_____

_____

_____

_____

_____

_____

11.3 Coordination, balance, reaction time and agility (p142–143)

These underpin how well you perform skills.

11.3.1 If you are coordinated you are likely to be more skilful in your performances. **What is coordination?**

Coordination is _____

_____

_____

_____

11.3.2 If you are balanced when static or moving you are likely to be more skilful in your performances. **What is balance?**

Balance is _____

_____

_____

_____

11.3.3 If your reaction times are good then you are likely to be more skilful in your performances. **What is reaction time?**

Reaction time is_____

_____

_____

_____

11.3.4 If you are agile you are likely to be more skilful in your performances. **What is agility?**

Agility is _____

_____

_____

_____

11.4 Factors to consider when learning skills for sports (p143–149)

The stages of learning (143–144)

Learning can be said to take place in three stages. They are the cognitive stage, the associative stage and the autonomous stage.

11.4.1 Match the following **phrases** to the appropriate **stage of learning**. Use the table below.

Performing automatically
Working out what to do
Few mistakes
Refining technique
Movements are efficient and effective
In the groove
Beginner stage
Feel lost
Confident

Movements are not efficient nor effective
Intermediate stage
Technique mastered
Anxious and lack confidence
Thinking a lot about technique
Lots of mistakes
Movements are more efficient and effective
In control
Fewer and fewer mistakes

Practising a lot
Wayward
More confident
More in control
Advanced stage
Coordinated
Coordination poor
Coordination improving
Getting into the groove

Cognitive stage	Associative stage	Autonomous stage

Guidance and learning (p144–145)

You can learn the techniques of a skill through visual guidance, verbal guidance or physical/manual guidance.

11.4.2 Visual guidance is _____

_____

_____

11.4.3 Verbal guidance is _____

_____

_____

11.4.4 Physical/manual guidance is _____

_____

_____

11.4.5 The method that works best can depend on the learner. **Explain** this.

_____

_____

_____

_____

_____

Practice and learning (p145–147)

11.4.6 Why is practice important in learning a skill?

_____

_____

_____

_____

11.4.7 State the **type of practice** that the following examples best demonstrate.

Example	Type of practice
Practising taking penalties without a goalkeeper	
Practising set shots in basketball from the same spot	
Practising visualising yourself performing the tennis serve	
Practising the run-up for long jump	
Practising how to deal with situations that may arise	
Practising the throw-up for a tennis serve	
Practising where dribbling is not allowed in playing basketball	
Practising shot selection in badminton for different situations	
Practising a forward roll	
Practising the options possible for hits/taking free kicks	
Practising in different situations	
Practising that can be done anywhere	
Practising where no long kicks are allowed in Gaelic football	
Practising breaststroke, then leg kick only, then breaststroke	
Practising a chest pass in netball	
Practising long jump, then the take-off, then the long jump	

You can have a continuous block of practice or spaced practice over a number of weeks.

11.4.8 A continuous block of practice is more suited to learners who _____

_____

_____

11.4.9 Spaced practice over a number of weeks is more suited to learners who _____

_____

_____

Feedback and learning (p148)

You need feedback on your performances.

11.4.10 You can receive **intrinsic** feedback and **extrinsic** feedback. What is the difference?

_____

_____

_____

_____

_____

_____

11.4.11 You can receive **knowledge of results** and **knowledge of performance**. Which of these two provides information on the quality of the performance?

_____

Arousal and learning (p148–149)

There is an optimum zone of arousal.

11.4.12 Explain one **way** by which your **level of arousal** could be **raised**.

_____

_____

_____

_____

_____

11.4.13 Explain one **way** by which your **level of arousal** could be **lowered**.

_____

_____

_____

Time To Spare?

If you have finished this section and are waiting for others to finish, try the wordsearch.

b	o	f	e	e	d	b	a	c	k	c	p	b	c	r	o
b	a	s	i	c	v	i	s	u	a	l	l	i	k	s	e
b	a	x	m	n	i	s	s	s	o	x	n	s	o	c	c
t	a	e	k	b	t	t	o	s	s	l	a	m	b	v	r
s	l	l	i	p	e	r	c	e	p	t	u	a	l	e	c
e	a	p	a	l	t	l	i	a	n	i	n	u	x	t	p
i	c	m	o	n	e	a	a	n	r	t	m	t	s	n	e
f	i	o	s	t	c	o	t	b	s	p	r	o	l	u	r
r	s	c	n	c	h	e	i	o	r	i	a	n	t	i	f
g	y	n	o	s	n	l	v	u	n	e	c	o	l	o	o
n	h	e	n	i	i	i	e	s	b	a	v	m	i	h	r
h	p	t	g	u	q	s	i	p	g	r	k	o	m	e	m
i	i	a	q	o	u	c	t	i	l	o	p	u	s	c	a
v	i	e	e	y	e	c	l	e	s	r	i	s	n	c	n
y	c	g	y	n	o	i	t	a	n	i	d	r	o	o	c
e	a	e	v	i	t	i	n	g	o	c	f	c	m	i	e
s	i	t	n	y	q	y	s	l	r	g	y	a	l	o	c

skill   extrinsic   coordination
goal   complex   associative
consistency   technique   verbal
basic   agility   intrinsic
motor   task   practice
equilibrium   performance   perceptual
visual   feedback   balance
physcial   cognitive   autonomous

11.5 Planning a safe, appropriate and effective workout to develop skills

Intention of the workout *(p150)*

Imagine you have watched a beginner perform a number of times and you have identified strengths and weaknesses in the performance of skills.

11.5.1 What should be the main intentions or objectives for workouts on skills?

___

11.5.2 What can happen in skill-related workouts if there are not clear learning intentions or objectives?

___

Analysis and evaluation of performance of an identified skill *(p150)*

15.5.3 What do you need to know to **assess how well** an individual performs a skill?

___

11.5.4 It is through observing the skill being performed that you identify areas of weakness in the performance of the skill. What are the advantages of using a digital camcorder to record the performances of a skill?

___

___

___

___

Teaching/coaching a skill *(p151)*

11.5.5 To teach/coach a skill you need to know the 'full marks' model for that skill. Describe the methods that can be used to communicate the 'full marks' model to the learners.

___

___

___

11.5.6 The most appropriate method for communicating the 'full marks' model depends on the skill and the learner. Explain this.

___

___

___

___

___

___

11.5.7 Complete the following paragraph by entering the appropriate words.

| feedback | verbal | perform | practices | visual |
| technique | pressure | demonstrate | grasp | mental |

The challenge is to use _____ and _____ guidance to give the learner a _____ image of how to

_____ the correct _____ of the skill (the 'full marks' model). You then provide the learner with

opportunities to _____ to you the correct technique without being under any _____. You observe

the learner's performances and provide _____. The learner is then given further opportunities to demonstrate

to you the correct technique of the skill. Once there is sufficient _____ of the technique, it can be performed in

selected _____.

11.5.8 Choose **one skill** from an activity that you have done for GCSE PE. For that skill write down the verbal guidance that you would give to a learner so that they would have a clear mental image of how to perform the techniques of that skill.

_____

_____

_____

_____

_____

_____

Selection of practices *(p151–152)*

The type and difficulty of the practice used depends on the complexity of the skill and on the stage that an individual is at in learning it.

11.5.9 Practices must suit the stage of learning. **Explain** how you would apply this to the three stages of learning.

Cognitive stage _____

_____

_____

_____

Associative stage _____

_____

_____

_____

Autonomous stage _____

_____

_____

_____

Giving feedback (p152–153)

11.5.10 'Knowledge of performance' provides the most helpful extrinsic feedback. What information do you give with this category of extrinsic feedback?

_____

_____

_____

_____

11.5.11 Briefly describe the methods that you can use to **give feedback** to a learner.

_____

_____

_____

_____

_____

Once you have sound technique in place, practices are important. It is practising a skill with sound technique that develops and forms a clear and precise memory of the skill.

Organisation (p153)

11.5.12 For badminton practices, why is it useful to have someone who is at the autonomous stage to help someone who has just moved from the cognitive stage to the associative stage of learning.

_____

_____

_____

_____

_____

_____

_____

11.5.13 Read the example for planning a workout to develop skill on pages 154–156. Use the five steps from 'Evaluation of workouts to develop skills' on pages 156 and 157 to evaluate this workout. Provide evidence to support your evaluation.